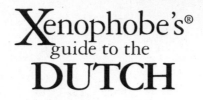

Xenophobe's®
guide to the
DUTCH

Rodney Bolt

Oval Books

Xenophobe's Guides
5 St. John's Buildings
Canterbury Crescent
London SW9 7QH
United Kingdom

Telephone: +44 (0)20 7733 8585
E-mail: info@ovalbooks.com
Web site: www.xenophobes.com

First printed 1995
New editions 1999, 2008
Reprinted/updated 1996, 1998, 1999, 2000,
2001, 2002, 2004, 2005, 2006, 2007, 2008,
2010, 2011

Editor – Catriona Tulloch Scott
Series Editor – Anne Tauté

Cover designer – Jim Wire & Vicki Towers
Printer – CPI Antony Rowe, Wiltshire

ePub ISBN: 9781908120274
Mobi ISBN: 9781908120281
Print ISBN: 9781906042288

Contents

The Dutch population is 16.5 million – compared with 5 million Danes, 5 million Scots, 10 million Belgians, 47 million Spanish, 52 million English, 64 million French, 82 million Germans and 313 million Americans.

The Netherlands is half the size of Scotland, not quite as large as Denmark, and could fit into Spain 12 times.

Nationalism & Identity

Forewarned

The Dutch character is inextricably bound up with the Dutch landscape. The Netherlands is so flat that even the black and white cows stand silhouetted against the skyline. Consequently the Dutch are used to distant horizons and lots of light. Openness, freedom and vision are fundamental. Few Dutch people could be happy living in a forest. When one of the Netherlands' most famous novelists sent his parents on their first trip to Switzerland as a present for their 50th wedding anniversary, he was disconcerted to discover that they had returned home after only a day or two. His mother had been bitterly disappointed. She had no view from her hotel window, she explained, there were mountains in the way.

> **The Dutch landscape is mild and uneventful. Intrusions, such as trees, occur in orderly lines.**

The Dutch landscape is mild and uneventful. Intrusions, such as trees, occur in orderly lines and patterns. Water, which threatens to overrun the whole country, is neatly channelled into straight canals. Control and moderation are important in behaviour too. "High trees catch a lot of wind," the Dutch warn. They describe excess in terms of *overvloed*, a 'flooding over' – as if the waters had burst the dykes. In the Netherlands, extravagant people don't waste money, they 'spill' it.

The Netherlands is light, but not bright – a world of greens, greys and browns. This colour scheme is repeated in the cities, where buildings are mainly of brown brick, and local bye-laws often state that residents must paint their front doors in the same shade of green. When Van Gogh forsook his native country for the brighter, bumpier regions of the south of France, he left off painting in the cosy, gravy browns of 'The Potato Eaters', took to gaudier hues, and went mad.

> **❝ The Dutch pride themselves on their tolerance and flexibility: qualities which, in addition to carrying moral kudos, are good for business. ❞**

How they see themselves

From the comfort of their immaculate sitting rooms the Dutch may acknowledge that they are the cleanest people on earth, are thrifty, have a canny head for business, an unparalleled facility with languages, an unequalled ability to get along with one another and an inimitable charm. But they will be far too modest, unless pushed, to admit publicly that all this makes them somewhat superior to other nations.

Above all, the Dutch pride themselves on their tolerance and flexibility: qualities which, in addition to carrying moral kudos, are good for business. The blanket of benevolence is not a woolly liberal one, but is woven from the sound stuff of commerce. It is quite thick enough to cover niggling inconsistencies, such as a secret mistrust of Moroccans, distaste at alien cooking smells from the apartment downstairs, or fury at foreigners who wobble inexpertly on bicycles, blocking the way for others.

How others see them

Most nations regard the Dutch as organized and efficient – rather like the Germans, but not as awesome. One can hardly be frightened, the reasoning goes, of a nation of rosy-cheeked farmers who live in windmills and have clogs at the bottom of the wardrobe, tulips in the garden and piles of round cheese in the larder.

But the Dutch also have a reputation for being opinionated, stubborn, and incorrigibly mean. The Belgians go even further, and complain that their neighbours are downright devious in business

> **66 Most nations regard the Dutch as organized and efficient – rather like the Germans, but not as awesome. 99**

affairs. Generally, though, other nations see them as forthright to a fault. Dutch frankness completely overwhelms more reticent peoples such as the Japanese who find the Dutch the rudest and most arrogant of the Europeans they do business with – though they are impressed by Dutch acumen as traders. 'Where a Dutchman has passed, not even the grass grows any more,' say the Japanese.

The English survey the Dutch with guarded approval, as the closest any Continentals come to the sacrosanct state of being English. Such chumminess has not always prevailed. In the 17th century these two seafaring nations were at each other's throats. An English pamphlet raged: 'A Dutchman is a Lusty, Fat, Two-legged Cheeseworm. A Creature that is so addicted to eating Butter, Drinking Fat and Sliding [skating] that all the world knows him for a slippery fellow.' The English language gained a whole new list of pejoratives, including 'Dutch courage' (booze-induced bravery), 'Dutch comfort' ('things could be worse') and 'Dutch gold' (fake). Nowadays there is an echo of this attitude in the tendency of some people (especially customs officers) to see the Dutch as a nation of drug-dazed pornographers. But on the whole the Dutch score top marks for cabling BBC television to every home in the land and speaking English without flinching or causing much of a flinch.

> **66 In the 17th century an English pamphlet raged: 'A Dutchman is a Lusty, Fat, Two-legged Cheeseworm. 99**

How they would like others to see them

The Dutch would like to be held up as The Ultimate Europeans. To this end they have assiduously assimilated so much from the nations around them that they have almost done away with their own cultural identity. This means that most people find something familiar about the Dutch, which guarantees that everybody likes them.

That the Netherlands is the small boy in the class of Europe doesn't unduly bother either its residents or its politicians. By making enough noise and having an opinion about everything, even a small boy can be noticed. With luck he might even become class captain – a job that, with his insider's knowledge of unfairness and oppression, he knows he can do more justly than some other class members he might care to mention. Especially those with a history of bullying.

> **f Most people find something familiar about the Dutch, which guarantees that everybody likes them. ™**

How they see others

Despite the fact that they have for centuries been edging their country towards the British Isles, the Dutch feel ambivalent about the British. They are surprised that these rather puny islanders, who clam up when one talks to them about sex, somehow manage to write such good books. They also see the English as cottagey and a bit twee, but adore their Marks & Spencer's underwear and are amazed that such an uptight nation could produce such elegant and practical designs. In some circles, English style is viewed as the ultimate chic. Tweeds, waxed jackets and pinstripes are sported by the discreetly rich, and those who aspire to that status.

Like most of their European neighbours, the Dutch

> **66 Forthrightness may be a virtue, but extravagantly flaunting your emotions smacks of lack of control. 99**

lap up the trappings of American culture, while dismissing its perpetrators as being empty-headed and loud. Road movies, especially, appeal to the Dutch sense of freedom and openness. The lost hitchhiker look is a popular Dutch fashion.

France and Italy may be suitable places to holiday, but the Dutch view their inhabitants with a twinge of disapproval. The French are too frivolous to win the lasting admiration of a nation that has Calvin in its bones, and besides, say the Dutch, they are obstructionists with no skill at negotiation. A nation that allows its farmers to pile turnips on the motorway must be viewed with some scepticism.

Forthrightness may be a virtue, but extravagantly flaunting your emotions smacks of lack of control – and so the Italians (and most other Mediterraneans) join the ranks of the 'tolerated-but-not-quite-as-good-as-us'. A notch below these come the nationalities whose religious or political customs are seen as intolerant. Such peoples are most emphatically not tolerated – intolerance of intolerance being quite permissible. Using this argument, an anti-Islamist party made massive gains in the 2010 general elections, to become the third largest in parliament, beating even the previous governing party.

Of all the European nations, the Dutch admire the Swiss. Their country is spotless, their banks unassailable and their personal bank accounts are secret.

Special relationships

Even the accommodating Dutch have their limits. The first barrier that Dutch tolerance comes up against is the German border. There is no one more likely to rouse the Dutch from their customary cheerfully benign state than a German. The Dutch see the Germans as arrogant, noisy, rigid and intolerant – everything in fact that the Dutch are not. They are wary of a nation that shows such a passion for living in forests. But usually they don't even bother to try and

66 The first barrier that Dutch tolerance comes up against is the German border. 99

explain. They simply do not like Germans. Telling a Dutch person that their language seems very similar to German is unlikely to benefit your relationship. Remarking that the two nations seem rather alike in many ways will probably get you thrown out of the house.

Should a German asks for directions in a Dutch city,

a Dutch person may well point to the border or the nearest international railway station. Or perhaps retort "First give my bike back!", and burst into gales of laughter. This is an in-joke referring to the fact that the Germans confiscated all bicycles during the Second World War. The implication is: first return the cycle you stole from my family, and only then might I feel obliged to help you. Dutch people of all ages make this joke. They do it even if their parents are not old enough to have experienced the Occupation. Anything to knock the Germans down a notch or two.

> **66 Though they really admire the way they enjoy life, the Dutch regard the Belgians as laughably dim. 99**

The Netherlands' southern border also presents a bit of a stumbling block. Apart from the Afrikaners in South Africa and the inhabitants of a few scattered ex-colonies, the Belgians are the only people in the world who speak a language anything like Dutch. One might think that this would endear their southern cousins to the Netherlanders, but (though they really admire the way they enjoy life) the Dutch regard the Belgians as laughably dim, and fit only for derision:

"What's written on the bottom of a Belgian milk bottle?" "Open other end."

"What's written on the bottom of a Belgian swimming pool?" "No Smoking."

"Why are Belgian glasses square?"

"So they don't leave a round mark on the table."

In the Netherlands itself, the inhabitants of the most southerly province of Limburg (whose capital is Maastricht) are saddled with the reputation of being stupid, hence:

"What happens when a person from Maastricht goes to live in Belgium?"

"The average IQ of both nations rises."

Character

Open minds

One of the most original of Dutch traits is the national tendency to let in a little evil in order to keep the big evil out. This admirable and astute approach is visible, for example, in the way they manage waterlocks: when tidal pressure builds up on the dykes, a controlled amount of water is allowed through so as to relieve the greater water pressure which might otherwise cause havoc. Drugs and various other sins are treated in exactly the same way: let a manageable amount in, so as to prevent whole-sale degeneracy or wanton excess.

> **One of the most original of Dutch traits is the tendency to let in a little evil in order to keep the big evil out.**

This explains the distribution of free needles to heroin addicts, prisoners' conjugal rights, teenage abortion on request, and coffee shops that sell marijuana over the counter. The Dutch even tolerate people's insistence on calling their country 'Holland', when Holland is in fact a province of the Netherlands. (Or to be precise North Holland and South Holland are two provinces of the Netherlands, so Holland on its own doesn't exist at all.)*

> **66 Tolerance is not simply a virtue, it is a national duty. 99**

Visitors may gape at a rollerblader wearing nothing but a silver G-string as he glides through the Saturday morning shoppers, but the Dutch will walk by unruffled – even if, secretly, they are as shocked as everyone else. Tolerance is not simply a virtue, it is a national duty. With 370 people for every square kilometre, the Netherlands is Europe's most densely populated country. If the Dutch didn't forgive – or at least ignore – each other's foibles and peculiar inclinations, life itself would become intolerable. Tolerance is really pragmatism in disguise, and so counts as a good, solid Protestant value.

But there is a hitch. The Dutch will tolerate anything – provided it does not infringe upon their own freedom – unless it smacks a little too much of

---

*However, even the Dutch seem to have abandoned the struggle – their football call is "Hup, Holland!".

dangerous abandon or lack of control. A deep respect for people's freedom to live their own lives, in their own way, is as Dutch as dykes and windmills. The Dutch place the bounds to behaviour along lines that reflect a tacit understanding of just how far you can go before knocking down the invisible walls of privacy and personal liberty. Life behind these walls is at the same time public, yet nobody else's business. Dutch Tolerance does not mean *acceptance*. Beneath the surface of dutiful tolerance may well lurk a deep antagonism – to men who hold hands, perhaps, or women who wear veils. Whether it is acted on depends on whether transgressors are seen to be stepping over the wall and disrupting a Dutch way of life.

> **66 A deep respect for people's freedom to live their own lives, in their own way, is as Dutch as dykes and windmills. 99**

Judging where the boundaries lie is never easy. In the Netherlands on Remembrance Day, the two-minute silence for the dead of the two World Wars is generally and movingly observed. Trams, cars and people come to a halt. A visitor was struck by the expressions around him when an immigrant family, unaware of the reverence of the occasion, continued on their way talking noisily amidst the stillness and the sea of solemn faces. It was clear that the Dutch were in a quandary: to scold the foreign refugees would seem intolerant; they had broken the unwritten rules, but then how were they to know? Should they be told? But to inter-vene would infringe their own cultural freedom. And so the reasoning tumbled on, leading to somersaults of moral confusion – though to a growing segment of the Dutch population the dilemma is not so much about telling the foreigners to shush, as about whether they should be there in the first place.

Open curtains

The Dutch are open about everything. Preserved veg-etables come in glass jars rather than in tins. Lavatories have a shelf in the bowl, ensuring that even your internal workings are open to daily inspection (the one German invention the Dutch have taken to with relish).

> **❝ The Dutch are open about everything. They build houses with big windows and do not draw their curtains at night. ❞**

To assure their neighbours, and themselves, that they have nothing to hide, the Dutch build houses with big windows and do not draw their curtains at night. You can watch your neighbours' television, see what they are having for dinner, note whether they shout at their children and fervently exercise your powers of tolerance if you notice anything untoward.

Clean windows are the primary concern of any householder, and rooms are lit with a subtle chiaroscuro that presents a cosy picture to the street at night. Rather than draw the blinds, people whose houses open directly on to the street hang little screens made out of wooden-framed doilies in the windows, or stick narrow strips of clouded plastic to the glass. These are positioned to avoid tiresome eye-contact with passers-by, while still leaving the room open to public view.

People keep their curtains open to reassure the world that they are not doing anything shameful – or that they are

> **❝ When openness spreads to personal relationships, it leads to a perfect frankness. ❞**

completely unashamed of anything that they might be getting up to. But no Dutch person would dream of staring in at the windows. That would be an invasion of privacy. Curiously, it was a Dutch television company that first came up with the idea for *Big Brother*, the show that allows millions to be Peeping Toms, ogling at the intimacies of a group of people made to live together in a single house. This is the ultimate expression of Open Curtains, while spicing things up by breaking the paramount social taboo.

When this openness spreads to personal relationships, it leads to a perfect frankness that other nations may find disarming. If you are suffering from a particularly unfortunate haircut, an English friend might tactfully suggest that you wear that nice hat you bought last week. A Dutch person will ask you what on earth has happened to your hair.

13

Gezelligheid

Gezelligheid is the Dutch nirvana. Dictionaries ineptly translate *gezelligheid* as 'cosiness'. The German *Gemütlichkeit* comes a little nearer the mark, but that nation has order rather than conviviality as its ultimate goal. A Dutch historian has described g*ezelligheid* as 'partly a sort of cosiness and partly a living togetherness'. The mood in a neighbourhood café on a cold winter's afternoon is *gezellig*; a mother will call "Keep it *gezellig*!" if she hears her offspring becoming dangerously boisterous; a popular Dutch beer is advertised as 'guaranteed *gezellig*'. Rather than switch on the lights at twilight, a family will light a few candles, make a pot of coffee and sit looking out of their large clean window, suffusing themselves in *gezelligheid*.

> **❝ Life runs according to a subtle decorum. The Dutch don't say "What will the neighbours think?", but "Think of the neighbours!" ❞**

Living on top of each other as they do, the Dutch have discovered that the best way to get on is by making sure that everything is always *gezellig*. Life runs according to a subtle decorum. The Dutch don't say "What will the neighbours think?", but "Think of the neighbours!"

If you drive in the wrong direction up a quiet one-way street at two o'clock in the morning and meet the police head-on, they will probably pull over and let you pass. There are more important things to do than arresting someone who is doing so little harm. Besides, it would not be *gezellig*. Dutch tolerance is the moral face of *gezelligheid*.

Going Dutch

This is the nation that sells scrapers for getting the last remnants of the film of buttermilk from the inside of the bottle. The Dutch 'think with their pockets'. Parsimony is not an embarrassment, but a virtue. On trains you will see people encouraging their dogs to sit in their holdalls. This is because the dog then qualifies as 'hand baggage' rather than 'accompanying pet', and so is not eligible for a ticket. Rather than objecting, ticket inspectors regard this as admirable ingenuity.

> 66 'Going Dutch' was invented so that the Dutch could sit back and enjoy their coffee in peace without worrying about who was going to pick up the bill. 99

Expenditure is acceptable only when there is hope of realising a profit. The Dutch have a saying that 'the cost comes before the benefit'. Otherwise it's a case of *elk dubbeltje omdraaien* – turning over each coin twice before even thinking of spending it. 'Going Dutch' was invented so that the Dutch could sit back and enjoy their coffee in peace, without worrying about who was going to pick up the bill.

Yes, but...

For the Dutch, the other side of the question is as important as the question itself. Dialogue is the lubricant of tolerance, and the essential ingredient of dialogue is "Yes, but...". Squatters enter into dialogue with landlords and the city council, and drug dealers sit down to cosy chats with the police. Opposition is by negotiation rather than confrontation. It's more *gezellig*.

Having an opinion

Discourse on death or sexual deviance may cause other nations to squirm, euphemize or change the topic, but will have the Dutch frankly and happily airing an opinion. When they find themselves somewhat shocked by a theme, then tolerance will start firing on all cylinders and the conversation will hurtle on. If, after a while, nobody has voluntarily come up with an alternative opinion, the conversation will momentarily pause, someone will politely offer a "Yes, but..." or an "On the other hand...", and talk will resume in a new direction. Tolerance requires that issues be examined from all sides.

> **Tolerance requires that issues be examined from all sides.**

One topic is an exception to this rule – your income. Discussing what you earn and how much you spend on your rent, your clothes or your car will elicit far deeper disapproval than admitting what you might get up to in bed. The only time that personal finances are considered in any way suitable material for conversation is after a visit to the dentist. Then everyone can join in the talk about bridges and crowns and the horrific size of their bills.

> **66 Discussing what you earn or how much you spend will elicit far deeper disapproval than admitting what you might get up to in bed. 99**

Acceptable Dutch conversation-warmers include football and the weather. The patterns are the same in either case: a brief comment on the present state of play, a remark or two about the previous week's offerings and speculation about things to come. Then you can move on to general analysis and the stating of opinions.

Beliefs & Values

Merchant values

The Dutch are traders at heart, and have a few centuries of outstanding success in the field to back up their belief that business rules. '*Handel is handel*' – trade is trade – is considered a justifiable excuse for any apparent hypocrisy, be it selling mercury that poisons the workers in South American goldmines, or extending airport runways while at the same time deploring the effect of jets on the environment. When a 17th-century munitions dealer was accused of supplying the enemy he retorted: 'If we didn't sell to them, we couldn't afford to fight them.' This logic was considered acceptable then, and it still is today, when for example questions are raised about selling equipment to certain Middle-Eastern countries.

Somewhere in the shadows behind every diligent trader lurks the Protestant work ethic. The Dutch believe that they were all born miserable sinners, and that this world is a place to work and suffer in.

They have even had to make their own land to live on, reclaiming it from the sea. 'God created the earth, but the Dutch made the Netherlands', the saying goes. Later, because they are so tolerant, they will get to heaven – but that is unlikely to affect God's attitude one jot, and they will probably have to toil and sweat up there too. In the meantime, '*Arbeid adelt*' ('Work makes noble'), and 'Laziness is the devil's pillow'.

> 66 'God created the earth, but the Dutch made the Netherlands', the saying goes. 99

Calvin rules

Protestant values are so firmly planted in Dutch soil that it comes as a surprise to most people to find that 35% of the population are registered as Roman

Catholic. Traditionally, the Catholics occupy a patch in the south-east, while the rest of the country (including all the big cities) is mainly Protestant. But for centuries Calvinism has ruled with such a firm hand that even the Church of Rome has responded to its grip. Despite having separate schools and their own television station, it seems as if the Netherlands' Catholics are living behind a solidly built Protestant façade and show a good puritan penchant for hard work and sober living. Muslims are tolerated provided they do the same.

> **❝ For centuries Calvinism has ruled with such a firm hand that even the Church of Rome has responded to its grip. ❞**

In days of yore, Catholics were tolerated (of course), but had to worship inconspicuously, behind closed doors, in churches built to look like houses. Today, mosques suffer the same fate and are only just beginning (after some three decades posing to the outside world as homes or shopfronts) to poke the odd conspicuous minaret up into the skyline.

The Sabbath is the one day that the Dutch can stop working without too much of a conscience. Most dedicate their Sundays to tennis, watching football and walking the dog; but in some rural areas whole villages turn out en masse for church, walking hooked together two-by-two, wearing hats and their sober Sunday best and directing withering looks at anyone so frivolous as to ride a bicycle or mow the lawn.

The wagging finger

The spirit of tolerance does constant battle with the ghost of Calvin for control of the Dutch psyche. Few Dutch people go to church any more, but they don't need to. Inside every Hollander's head is a little pulpit containing a preacher with a *vermanende vinger*, a wagging finger. Laziness and immoderation are the main themes of his sermon. His business is to provide a nagging Protestant conscience. Often he is let loose to admonish the outside world.

> **66 Inside every Hollander's head is a little pulpit containing a preacher with a wagging finger. 99**

Dirty windows, behaviour that is not *gezellig* (lager louts and German tourists are the main culprits here) and flashy extravagance will all set a Dutch person's own finger wagging. But most of all the *vermanende vinger* is there to ensure respectability. The impulse towards becoming a good, solid citizen is irresistible. Even cannabis traders have formed an association that exercises quality control and ensures that members pay their taxes. The only thing that can severely inhibit the *vermanende vinger* is a powerful counter-impulse from the duty to be tolerant or the suggestion of financial profit.

Pillars of the community

The pillars of the Dutch Establishment are not individuals, but institutions. For centuries Dutch society rested firmly on the two pillars (*zuilen*) of the Protestant and Catholic churches. More recently, trendy socialist and ethnic columns have been added to the colonnade. There are still separate Protestant and Catholic universities, trades unions, television channels and political parties. People may nowadays treat them interchangeably, but to chip away at this segregation would be to invite dreadful collapse. In rural areas especially, the boundaries are still fiercely defended. A small village with a Protestant, a Catholic and a Montessori school may not have enough pupils to go round, but each establishment would sooner close down than merge with any of the others.

Oddly, this perception that society is made up of different *zuilen* goes hand-in-hand with the Dutch belief in tolerance: mutually exclusive world views need not be mutually destructive, but can jointly prop up a sturdy *gezellige* whole.

> **The pillars of the Dutch Establishment are not individuals, but institutions.**

Zuilen are also very comforting. Building yourself into a *zuil* means that you don't have to get involved with the nitty-gritty of actually integrating with anything you consider foreign, but can still congratulate yourself on accepting it as a separate though essential part of society. The phenomenon is again becoming apparent in larger cities where whole areas of town, and even some schools, are silently labelled

'Moroccan' or 'Turkish' – or that Dutch hold-all word *allochtonen*, which theoretically should encompass all 'aliens', but in practice means only those who are not white. It was the descendants of Dutch settlers in South Africa who, similarly twisting the reasoning of *zuilen*, invented *Apartheid*.

Wealth and success

The pursuit of wealth is a favourite Dutch pastime, and accumulating money is a virtue. Spending it is a vice. The Dutch word *schuld* means both 'debt' and 'guilt'. A healthy bank balance may be proof that you are shouldering your earthly burden of hard work, but it's a private assurance.

Just as discussing one's salary is frowned upon, the Dutch consider a flashy display of worldly goods as extreme bad taste. When one national magazine published a list of the Netherlands' top ten richest people, they had to follow it the next week with an apology to one of the millionaires for placing him too high on the list.

> **66 Accumulating money is a virtue. Spending it is a vice. The Dutch word *schuld* means both 'debt' and 'guilt'. 99**

Wariness of showy excess extends to many levels. A leading Dutch executive was quoted as saying that he found the catering in Business Class of the national airline disagreeably over-the-top. He would be quite satisfied with a cheese roll and a glass of buttermilk.

This is not to say that the Dutch deny themselves material comfort. It is perfectly acceptable to surround yourself with *degelijke spullen* – good, sound objects that work efficiently. They may even be stylish, but never ostentatious. A modest Mercedes might pass muster; a Rolls Royce would

> **❝ The Dutch pride themselves on their egalitarian society. There may be a Queen, but she is a stolid upholder of respectable middle-class values. ❞**

raise a disapproving eyebrow. Even the grandest Dutch homes present a narrow, low-key façade to the street, but, in private behind it, stretch out into spacious rooms and secluded gardens.

Class

The Dutch pride themselves on their egalitarian, class-less society. There may be a Queen, but she is a stolid upholder of *burgelijke* (respectable middle-class) values rather than a fairytale monarch. Dutch citizens don't have to bow or curtsey to her, and she was 'invested' rather than crowned.

A tiny handful of old families, together with a selection of graduates from long-established universities, make up a small, self-supporting Old Boys' network that is spun through big business, banking and the diplomatic corps. The rest of the Netherlands belongs to a sprawling middle class that laughs at snobbery and gets along quite happily with itself. At one end of the spectrum are the university-educated professionals who watch English-language television on cable; at the other are the workers who soak up soaps and sensationalist magazines. But, unlike the British, they speak a mutually comprehensible language and play life by similar rules.

Obsessions

Coffee

Coffee is a national institution. The most significant classical Dutch novel is about coffee. A cup of coffee marks all goings out and comings in. It is the point around which friendships, funerals, birthdays and office life pivot. The average Dutch person gets through 144 litres of the stuff each year – that's 3.2 cups a day. It is the essential lubricant of *gezelligheid*.

> **Coffee is a national institution. The most significant Dutch novel is about coffee.**

In the Netherlands coffee is served black and strong enough to double the pulse rate. Coffee with milk is tolerated, but is considered to be almost another drink. The Dutch call it *koffie verkeerd*, literally 'coffee wrong'. Putting cream in coffee is seen as downright odd, though it is acceptable to add *koffie melk*, a kind of evaporated milk.

In cafés a cup of coffee comes complete with a small biscuit. This is as fundamental an accessory as sugar cubes or the little plastic cup of *koffie melk*. The Dutch nibble through more biscuits per annum than any other nation in Europe. The only explanation for their not being top of the coffee consumption league as well is that someone, somewhere, must be recycling used grains.

Neatness

A British magistrate, paying a visit to a Dutch home in the 17th century, was astonished when the housemaid plonked him down on the outside step, plucked off his muddy boots and carried him across the shining hall floor to her mistress's parlour. Around the same period a supper-less French cleric complained that the Dutch would sooner die of hunger than disturb the perfect symmetry of the sparkling crockery and glittering cauldrons in their kitchens.

> **Inside and out, the Netherlands appears clipped, scrubbed, washed, polished and freshly painted.**

Little has changed. Inside and out, the Netherlands appears clipped, scrubbed, washed, polished and freshly painted. Trees in the countryside are planted in lines, and the black-and-white cows are arranged in neat little groups. Battalions of street-sweepers and cleaning machines advance through the cities day and night.

Indoors, people scour, buff and tidy to meet the ideal set for them by the poised interiors painted by Old Masters such as Vermeer and Saenredam. Those who fail are accused of having a 'Jan Steen household', after the artist famed for his portrayal of chaotic and debauched tavern scenes.

> **66 Indoors, people scour, buff and tidy to meet the ideal set for them by the poised interiors painted by Old Masters. 99**

Just to make sure that householders toe the line, specially designated Environmental Police will poke through any garbage bags left outside the demarcated collection points, or deposited in the street on days other than specified collection days. If they come up with anything that has your address on it, you will receive a nasty letter, and possibly a fine.

New building designs have to be approved not only by town planners, but also by a *Schoonheids Commissie* (literally, 'Beauty Commission'). Rulings can be quite idiosyncratic: plans for a new passenger terminal for cruise ships (itself designed to resemble a ship at sea) were rejected because the 'waves' on part of the roof were going the wrong way.

Water

Over 40% of the Netherlands is below sea level, much of it land stolen from marshes, rivers and the ocean. The Dutch live with a constant sense of guilt about this. On one hand the situation is good for the Calvinistic psyche: the Dutch are the chosen people diligently battling against the tide, locked into a never ending and morally uplifting struggle merely to keep their heads above water. On the other hand, they live in fear of divine retribution for their cheek. The Almighty might threaten other nations with plagues and earthquakes, but He threatens the Dutch with inundation.

When floods do occur, the stream of refugees away from the stricken areas is countered by an equal but opposite flow of sightseers who will stand and watch the waters rising with the sort of titillated awe that other nations reserve for multiple pile-ups on motorways.

> **The Almighty might threaten other nations with plagues and earthquakes, but He threatens the Dutch with inundation.**

Bicycles

There are 16 million bicycles in the Netherlands – that's virtually one for everyone living there. Punks, grannies, students and company directors trundle through the cities and swoop in fleets out into the countryside (especially on National Cycling Day). Not only does nearly every road have an accompanying cycle path, but plans are afoot to build a number of 'Bicycle Highways' that will speed you between towns with nary a stop-sign nor traffic light to delay you.

The Dutch parliament employs its own resident bicycle repair man, and one Dutch university even has a Professor of Bicycling. Even the Dutch first family has a good grip on the handlebars. Queen Juliana had a royal *rijwiel* (literally: 'riding wheel'), and Queen Beatrix made her offspring cycle to school – like any other children in the country, except that the young princes were followed by a bevy of bodyguards, on bikes of their own.

> **❝ The Dutch Bicycle is a solid, black machine – more Miss Marple than Tour de France. ❞**

The Dutch Bicycle is a solid, black machine which you ride in a sit-up-and-beg position. More Miss Marple than Tour de France, a 'good' Dutch bicycle will have a frame that appears to be made of cast iron, on to which are fastened working parts of an astonishing variety of vintages. Once, the only part that could be guaranteed not to work (if it was there at all) was the front light. But police crackdowns on lightless cycles (at one point leading to over 500 fines being handed out in one evening on a single street corner in Amsterdam) have led to a begrudging change in attitude. However, whether it's on or off hardly matters as the first rule of the Dutch Highway Code is that even when riding without a light, in the middle of the night in the wrong direction up a one-way street, the cyclist is always right. Motorists are aware of this and take the necessary precautions.

To the Dutch mind the bicycle is more an extension of the body than a separate means of transport. People behave on bicycles as they would do if they were walking. Lovers cycle hand-in-hand. If it rains, cyclists put up their umbrellas and pedal on. They will exercise the dog by riding about with the frisky animal tripping alongside on the end of its lead.

On the other hand, the nation's severe drinking and driving laws lump cyclists together with car-drivers rather than pedestrians. A charge of being drunk in charge of a bicycle could result in the loss of your driver's licence.

> **Dutch mothers build up sturdy calves pedalling along with one child on the front, one on the back, and panniers stuffed with shopping.**

Bicycles may be built for one, but to the Dutch this seems an unnecessary restriction. Parents fit little seats – one to the crossbar and one to the back carrier – to transport their offspring. Dutch mothers build up sturdy calves pedalling along with one child on the front, one on the back, and panniers stuffed with shopping. A burly rugby forward apparently singing in a sweet soprano turns out to be masking a merry mite on the carrier behind him. Courting couples share a bike too, usually with the woman riding side-saddle on the carrier. One of the early lessons of adolescence is learning how far a girl's legs stick out. First dates invariably involve bruised knees.

Behaviour

The family

A glance at the entries in the Births column of a national newspaper reveals the Dutch veneration for their children: 'Born to Hans and Jiske, a new world citizen, Onno, 14/4/11.'

The Dutch family is the kernel of *gezelligheid* and an academy for learning the skills of negotiation and tolerance. The Dutch treat children with respect, and expect them swiftly to pick up the trappings of respectability. From an early age children learn to "Keep it *gezellig*" and conduct themselves in a way that doesn't ruffle the feathers of those that surround them. "Behave normally, that's mad enough" they are often told – and in the Netherlands this is usually true.

> **66 The Dutch treat children with respect, and expect them swiftly to pick up the trappings of respectability. 99**

The young are credited with the intelligence to make decisions about their lives. When planning changes to a local playground, a Dutch borough council will send questionnaires to children rather than to parents. Even situations where 'Mummy knows best' are open to negotiation. Complicated deals are struck in super-market aisles as dinner options are discussed, spinach and broccoli being traded off against strawberry ice-cream and extra biscuits.

The Dutch allow families to take on some adventurous shapes, and do so with warmth and verve. Granny and grandpa, sitting down to Christmas lunch with their eldest son, his boyfriend, their unmarried daughter and her children, make a cosier gathering than many a family unit complete with one parent of each sex

> **" The Dutch allow families to take on some adventurous shapes, and do so with warmth and verve. "**

and 2.5 noisome brats. The Netherlands was the first country in the world completely to legalise gay and lesbian marriage, and to allow the families thus formed to expand by adopting children.

Animals

An old Dutch commonplace holds that 'If a Hollander should be bereft of his pipe of tobacco, he could not blissfully enter heaven'. Nowadays, for 'pipe of tobacco' read 'dog'. In such a populous country, you would expect more compact pets – such as budgies, hamsters or goldfish – to be the norm, but it is the bounding, jolly, slobber-over-everything-and-defecate-everywhere mutt that is the Dutch person's best friend. There is no escape. Dogs have free-range over parks, shops, cafés and restaurants.

The national obsession with cleanliness suffers a serious blip when it comes to dogs' dirt. Pavements are turned into obstacle courses. For pedestrians it is a case of eyes down, forget window-shopping and leave your deep-tread soles at home. Paving stones painted with a picture of a squatting dog, an arrow and the words *In de Goot* (In the Gutter) are sniffed at and ignored. The people may be multi-lingual, but their dogs can't even read Dutch.

The elderly

Alongside dogs and children, elders occupy a prime place in the Dutch pantheon – and they are determined to stay there. The younger generation may be

> **66 Elders occupy a prime place in the Dutch pantheon – and they are determined to stay there. 99**

beginning to mutter about the 'grey plague', but they are firmly put in their place. Grey power sees to that: after a lifetime of toil, the '65-plus' brigade felt they deserved a bit of fun, formed their own political party, and succeeded in winning six seats in the national parliament. Unfortunately old age was about all they could agree on. A succession of quarrels split their ranks so now they stand as independents, and seek satisfaction in representing themselves and in voicing a lifetime's opinions.

When the elderly are not campaigning for better pensions, they may be found belting their lungs out in a 'grey' version of the Eurovision Song Contest, cycling about the countryside and generally having the time of their lives.

Eccentrics

It is difficult to become an eccentric in the Netherlands. Dutch tolerance means that all sorts of odd behaviour is simply redefined as normal. The cardinal rule is that all behaviour is tolerated so long as it not un-*gezellig* or bad for business. However, there is a strong sense that you should not upset the apple cart or stick your head above the parapet. It's just that the Dutch apple cart is sturdier, and the parapet is a little higher, than most other Europeans are used to – behave normally, that's mad enough...

Immigrants

The Netherlands has long been a haven for people who have begun to find the sea a little choppy in their own part of the world. As a nation of good traders, the Dutch knew that it was in their best interest to be flexible when it came to the finer points of religious or political belief. In earlier centuries Protestants fled to the Netherlands from Antwerp (bringing diamond-cutting skills), and Jews came from Portugal (complete with news of secret trade routes).

Today, Turks, Surinamese, Indonesians, Moroccans

and refugees from the Balkans – to name just a few – live alongside the homegrown Dutch. People from former colonies, especially those from Indonesia, are now part of the warp and weave of Dutch society, but for many of the others 'living alongside' is just what they do. The Dutch retreat into their *zuilen*, and pack the immigrants up into one of their own.

Everyone determinedly displays their tolerance of refugees and foreigners, and might even remark on how they have perked up local cuisine and added a dash of colour to some parts of town, adding that it is just that things are more *gezellig* within the neat confines of your own particular compartment. But in some of the corners of these separate drawers there are now ominous grumblings about how foreigners take up all the apartments and jobs, and how, accommodating though the Dutch would like to be, the Netherlands is, unfortunately, just too full. There is concern that the Dutch way of life is under threat. The crack in the carapace of the duty to be tolerant has widened, and people have become stricter in their definition of what it means to be Dutch.

The law requires those from foreign cultures to undergo a process of inburgering ('acclimitization', or, more literally, 'citizenization'). This involves not

> **People from former colonies, especially those from Indonesia, are now part of the warp and weave of Dutch society.**

only language courses, but also tuition on how different aspects of Dutch society function, and how to fit in. Foreigners must not integrate, but assimilate. It's an attempt to prevent messy foreign habits from straying too far from the Dutch norm.

Manners & Etiquette

Dutch manners have more to do with affability than rigid form. Their aim is to create a *gezellige* ambience, where everyone can relax and enjoy each other's company. Even so, there are pitfalls that can trap the unwary. You will know that you have fallen in a hole when the atmosphere suddenly cools. You may not be left in the dark for long. Dutch people will generally tell you exactly what it is that you have done wrong – then it's your turn to feel offended by their bluntness.

> **Dutch people will generally tell you exactly what it is that you have done wrong – then it's your turn to feel offended by their bluntness.**

Greetings

When meeting someone for the first time, the Dutch smile, shake hands and give their name. The handshake is a warm one, somewhere between the

35

German pumping iron and British brevity. Soon they will be addressing each other by first names rather than surnames, though not with the alacrity that Americans show in these matters. In the meantime they are summing each other up.

Colleagues and acquaintances stick to handshakes, which increase in duration and warmth if they approve of one another. Across the bridge, in the realms of friendship, handshaking gives way to the Dutch kiss – one on each cheek and a third thrown in for good measure. The Dutch shake hands or kiss on meeting and at parting, invariably, and regardless of permutations in gender.

> **The Dutch (of both sexes) exchange flowers for the flimsiest of reasons. Posies pass between them like pecks on the cheek.**

When greeting people in the Netherlands it is useful to have some props to hand, namely flowers and coffee. The Dutch (of both sexes) exchange flowers for the flimsiest of reasons. Posies pass between them like pecks on the cheek. The next step after greeting, if it is humanly possible in the circumstances, is to have a cup of coffee.

Gestures and insults

The waving about of arms is one aspect of foreign culture that the Dutch have not adopted, though a wagging forefinger in the face of extravagance, intolerance or laziness is an unsuppressible homegrown reflex. In moments of extreme ire, the wagging forefinger may bow to a straightened middle finger, or a tap of the forehead to question someone's sanity.

Verbally, the Dutch express their disgust by damning things on behalf of God, and they insult each other with liberal reference to genitalia and bodily functions. This abuse is sometimes hard to distinguish from affection. *Scheetje* (little fart) or *drolletje* (little turd) are both terms of tender endearment.

Fingers off

Dutch frugality restricts guests to just one piece of cake with their coffee. Acceptance of a second slice (in the rare event of your being offered one) will result in the same silent disapproval as would cataloguing your woes in response to an English person's formulaic "How are you?"

Helping yourself to olives or peanuts with your pre-dinner sherry will also cause brows to furrow. The distribution of such bounty is strictly the host's domain. If the Dutch are confronted with a hearty "Help yourself!"

> **❝ Dutch frugality restricts guests to just one piece of cake with their coffee. Acceptance of a second slice (in the rare event of your being offered one) will result in silent disapproval. ❞**

as a guest at some foreign dinner table, they will end up embarrassed, or hungry, or both.

With U or without U

As they glide along the scale from acquaintanceship into friendship, the Dutch drop *U* (the formal 'you') in favour of *je* and *jij*. They do this more readily than the Germans, and many younger Dutch people don't bother with *U* at all. But many bosses and elders still expect to be called *U*, even if the conversation is quite chummy. Most people pussyfoot around, sheltering behind complicated sentence structures, until someone innocently lets drop a *je*, bringing down the barriers.

> **66 In shops, being addressed as *U* rather than *je* is a sad indication that you have finally turned the corner into middle age. 99**

In shops, being addressed by the assistant as *U* rather than *je* is a sad indication that you have finally turned the corner into middle age. Thanks are also best expressed with a *U*. Dutch children are told to "thank with two words" – *dank u*, rather than *bedankt* (a cop-out which is short for 'you are thanked', conveniently leaving out the pronoun). Business letters should never be without *U*, and to begin a sentence in a letter with *Ik* ('I') shows an arrogance which is unacceptable.

Queuing

Queuing is an import to the Netherlands that has met with limited success. In busy banks and post offices queues may be controlled electronically by flashing numbers and slips of paper. People mill around disconsolately until their number comes up. In the absence of such technology they will stand in line, but the important factor is not so much the order of people in the queue as the gap between its first occupant and the person actually conducting business at the counter.

The Dutch deeply respect privacy, especially in financial affairs, and you are expected to leave at least a metre between you and whoever is taking out money or buying stamps. There is often a line drawn on the floor beyond which you may not trespass. In shops, queuing is a more abstract affair. On entering a shop the Dutch make a mental note of who was there before

> **66 The Dutch make a mental note of who was there before them. Shop assistants abnegate all responsibility, simply calling out "Who's next?" 99**

them. Shop assistants abnegate all responsibility, simply calling out "Who's next?", leaving it to the customers to assert their rights of precedence, which they do in no uncertain terms. When it comes to buses, trams and trains, then elbows, umbrellas and sheer bulk rule.

Culture

Mix and match

The Dutch are cultural magpies. They keep a beady eye on other people's cultural trends, and are swift to snap up sparkling new fashions. This means that rather than producing an indigenous culture, they have become voracious consumers of everyone else's – true Europeans, whose cultural fads and fancies know no borders. The Netherlands acts as a giant cultural sponge.

Dutch bookshelves are well stocked with volumes from Britain, Germany, America and France, often in the original languages. Foreign books are reviewed in the Dutch press long before the translations appear in print. Music from every corner of the globe blasts out of local stereos

> **Rather than producing an indigenous culture, the Dutch have become voracious consumers of everyone else's.**

(the Dutch own more CDs per capita than anyone else). Theatres fill up for German plays and British musicals, and audiences flock to see Spanish and Italian films. Even the Dutch national clichés are not entirely homegrown. Clogs are worn in other muddy northern climes, Delftware is an imitation of Chinese porcelain, and the tulip was brought from Turkey.

Four centuries ago, in the heady years of the Netherlands' Golden Age, Dutch artists (finding no market in a Protestant country for virgins and saints) took to portraying themselves and the people around them. The result was an accurate and intimate portrait of their life and times. Never again has Dutch art succeeded in being quite so Dutch.

The abstract artist Mondriaan – he preferred to drop the second 'a' in his surname to make it sound more French – who was inspired by the Dutch landscape to paint his blocks of vertical and horizontal lines, emigrated to America, and the world claimed his work. Today the Netherlands hosts more artists per square inch than anywhere else in Europe. Suburban gardens sprout curious bolted sculptures and the interiors of public buildings are adorned with unfathomable paintings. The larger cities have 'Art Libraries' which will loan you original artworks to display at home. These are the products of up-and-coming artists and have been paid for by the city council in what amounts to a back-door subsidy of modern art.

> **66 The Netherlands hosts more artists per square inch than anywhere else in Europe. 99**

True to their mercantile tradition, the Dutch excel at turning around other people's cultural products and adding to their value. The Royal Concertgebouw Orchestra has long ranked with the finest in the world, and is especially famed for its performances of works by Gustav Mahler, an Austrian composer.

The nation is also unabashed about poaching foreign talent to run its cultural institutions. At the turn of the millennium, the Concertgebouw Orchestra's resident conductor was Italian, the director of the Van Gogh Museum was a Scot, the national ballet troupe was run by a Canadian, and the opera company was headed by a Franco-Lebanese.

> **The spirit of adventure, innovation and delight in things different fuels Dutch architecture and design.**

The same spirit of adventure, innovation and delight in things different that fired the traders of the Dutch East India Company, now fuels Dutch architecture and design. Homeless students are accommodated in apartments converted from abandoned shipping containers; business parks on the edge of town sport office blocks zigzagging with odd edges and skew whiff lines, or shaped like running shoes. A non-plussed public is treated to zany public art such as a mass of synthetic fried eggs (with yolks the size of igloos) spread across a city square, and flashing neon lights that read Hahahahahahaha.

The press

The Dutch are avid readers of newspapers, mostly purchased by subscription and therefore delivered by post rather than bought from a newsagent. This means that newspapers are read more at home than on trams or trains. Many command family loyalties that last for generations – especially those like *Trouw* and *Het Parool* that grew out of the underground press which flourished during the Nazi Occupation.

Apart from *De Telegraaf* (a spicy broadsheet), newspapers tend to be sensible and unsensationalist. The sort of salacious curiosity that fills the British tabloid press is diluted in the Netherlands, where privacy is respected. Wild speculation and lurid storylines are the realm of the cheap colour magazines that are standard reading in laundrettes, hairdressers', snack bars and dentists' waiting rooms.

Cafés offer piles of magazines and daily papers, so that if you arrive early you can quickly gen up on an opinion to get you through the rest of the evening.

> **" Cafés offer piles of magazines and daily papers so you can quickly gen up on an opinion. "**

This reading matter also ensures that life can be *gezellig* even if you are alone. Nobody complains if you sit for an entire afternoon over one cup of coffee, devouring every paper and glossy magazine the café has to offer.

Literature

Literature is the one area where Dutch culture has remained an island, made inaccessible by a language incomprehensible to most other Europeans. Paradoxically, it is on this island that the Dutch cultural climate is at its healthiest. Everyone is writing a novel. Producers of television chat shows seem able to tap into an endless supply of writers. Old stalwarts of the genre, such as Frederick Hermans, manage first edition print runs of over 500,000, and even newcomers sell books in the tens of thousands. The English-speaking world is beginning to take note. Writers such as Cees Nooteboom, Arthur Japin and Harry Mulisch have met with some success in translation, and the vignettes painted by Simon Carmiggelt bring foreign readers as close as they can hope to be to the heart of *gezelligheid*.

> **66 Jip and Janneke – a boy and a girl who live next door to each other – first meet by rubbing noses through the hedge. 99**

The Dutch begin their raids on foreign culture at a young age. Winnie-the-Pooh and the inhabitants of Sesame Street are lined up alongside locals such as Jip and Janneke – a boy and a girl who live next door to each other and first meet by rubbing noses through the hedge. Jip and Janneke are healthily naughty, but are always learning about good neighbourliness and correct behaviour. They hold a special place in the nation's heart, and their silhouettes can be found everywhere from lavatory doors to coffee mugs.

Apart from Jip and Janneke, the world of Dutch children's literature is populated by unbearably saintly beings – from the boy who saves the world by keeping his finger in the dyke, to Dik Trom, a fat village lad with a heart of gold who always helps the blind and the poor. Dik may not be much to look at, but, on the inside – as his parents constantly remind everyone – "he's a special boy, and that's a fact". The Dutch grow up believing they are the European Dik Troms.

Leisure & Pleasure

Though hard work is a necessary burden, it is one lightly borne. The Dutch work fewer hours per year than anyone else in the Western world (1,340 on average, compared with 1,467 in Germany and 1,820 in America), and they are also the world leaders when it comes to the proportion of the labour force (33%) who prefer to get by on working just a few days a week.

Taking a break from this burden of hard work, the Dutch relax over a cup of coffee. On special occasions they may do this in each other's houses (arriving with the statutory bunch of flowers, and consuming the regulation single piece of cake), but mostly they meet in cafés. The local café is a sort of communal sitting room – cosy, cheery and

> **Though hard work is a necessary burden, it is one lightly borne. The Dutch work fewer hours per year than anyone else in the Western world.**

packed with people who have left their own sitting rooms (empty and pristine, with the curtains open for all to see).

The primary requirement for entry into café society is an opinion. Armed with at least one opinion, a Dutch person can wile away a whole evening, relatively cheaply, locked in endless verbal battle over a cup of coffee, or – as the evening progresses – a slim glass of beer. Only an important football match, bursting into life on the television in the corner, can interrupt the flow.

> **“ Armed with at least one opinion, a Dutch person can wile away a whole evening, relatively cheaply, locked in endless verbal battle over a cup of coffee. ”**

When it comes to 21st-century leisure activities, the Dutch lag behind other nations – not because they are old-fashioned, but because it costs too much. On average, American games players each fork out Euros 113 for their pastime annually, and those in Belgium 121, while Dutch gamers manage just a measly 64.

Holidays

The Dutch consider a break from their native climate as essential to their health and mental stability, and emphasize the absolute necessity to well-being of 'Vitamin V' ('V' is for vacation). They prefer to take their holidays where they can soak up the sun, and so head for the hills of France, or the sunny coasts of Greece or Spain. The success of a Dutch holiday is calculated by the resultant depth of tan and the number of days on which it did not rain.

Even people on social security get an annual holiday allowance so that they can go and lie in the sun somewhere and recover from the stress of being unemployed. This works by Social Security paying its clients less than their prescribed allowance, implementing an enforced savings regime which turns into the holiday nest egg (with the authorities, of course, pocketing the interest the money has earned in the meantime). And if the workers succumb to bouts of *overspanning* (literally 'over-strain') when the going gets tough, a supportive note from the doctor allows the poor dears months, in some cases years, off work at near full-pay to recover.

> **The Dutch prefer their holiday to be as Dutch as possible. The surest way of achieving this is to take your home along with you.**

But the trek across the borders to sunnier climes is where any thought of adventure stops. In all respects other than weather, the Dutch prefer their holiday to be as *gezellig* and as Dutch as possible. The surest way of achieving this is to take your home along with you: there are nearly half a million caravans in the Netherlands. Sometimes whole neighbourhoods will set off together to create a *gezellige* corner of some foreign campsite that is forever Holland.

Caravanning has the additional advantage of being cheap. Even if they are lashing out on a holiday apartment, a Dutch family will be sure to fill the boot of their car with sacks of potatoes and other sensible Dutch provisions to protect their stomachs and pockets against the onslaughts of foreign fare, and ensure that they will not need to spend money along the way. At the beginning of summer you may even see signs in supermarkets urging customers to stock up before they set off for expensive foreign shores. The French complain that the Dutch even bring their own *water* with them. (This frugality is not restricted to campers. At one time The Gambia implemented a ban on Dutch tourists because they brought all their own food and contributed nothing to the local economy.)

66 At the beginning of summer you may even see signs in supermarkets urging customers to stock up before they set off for expensive foreign shores. **99**

"Yes, but..." (someone will point out), on the other hand, something of the Golden Age spirit of adventure remains. The force that centuries ago drove the Dutch to explore unknown regions of the globe still whisks them off and deposits them in far-flung places. Go on a lonely adventure climb in the Himalayas, or a canoeing trip along a remote tropical river, and the couple that come walking out of the distance, with all the *degelijke* (absolutely correct) gear, guide books in three languages, and speaking the local lingo perfectly, will be Dutch.

Sport

Most Dutch people seem satisfied with the daily exercise they get cycling, though a people surrounded by so much water are understandably good at swimming, notching up many an Olympic Gold.

In winter many take to skating. When it gets really cold, people sharpen their blades and talk of nothing else but the *elfstedentocht*, a marathon that takes place on the canals and waterways between eleven towns in Friesland. The frisson of anticipation as to whether the freeze will be widespread enough is almost as exciting as the race itself – which is just as well, as it is hardly ever cold enough to hold the *elfstedentocht*.

> **"A people surrounded by so much water are understandably good at swimming."**

Faced with their flat terrain, the Dutch have come up with some sports of their own. Members of the Dutch Mountaineering Club, acting out of desperation, spend their weekends scaling the sides of tall buildings or specially constructed (and commercially very profitable) 'climbing walls'. Hundreds of others opt for 'horizontal mountain climbing', i.e., wading thigh deep through the black, sucking mud off the Frisian coast. This they do for hours on end, before packing up and returning home. Early in August you can witness another home-grown pastime – pole sitting. Men sit on poles in the North Sea until they fall off. The last one to do so is the winner. Endurance of discomfort rescues such sports from any un-Calvinistic tendency towards frivolity.

> **66 Important football matches have been known to cause city council sessions to adjourn. 99**

After a good solid Dutch meal, nothing is better than to venture outdoors for a little '*uitwaaien*' (a 'blow out'), a walk in the wind for fun. When it comes to watching other people braving the elements and pitting their strength against each other, they favour football above all sports. Important matches have been known to cause city council sessions to adjourn, and support-ers to celebrate victories with officially sanctioned street parties. During the season, football eclipses the weather as a topic of conversation, and the remote con-trol unit gathers dust behind the sofa as the television stays stuck on the sports channel.

Television

The Netherlands has one of the oldest and most com-prehensive cable television networks in Europe. Nearly every household in the country has at its fingertips English, German, French, Belgian and Italian national stations, and a range of local and speciality channels – a veritable feast from which to pick and choose with relish. This suits their cultural make-up perfectly. Cable television is the modern expression of what the Dutch have been doing for centuries. They are the world's most adept cultural zappers.

The Dutch stations offer a mixed diet of foreign films, tacky game shows, over-acted soaps and talk shows. Watching

> **66 Watching people ponder, argue and opine appeals to the nation, so talk shows notch up high ratings. 99**

people ponder, argue and opine appeals to the nation, so talk shows notch up high ratings. The most popular ones are filmed live from cafés – an on-screen reflection of what the Dutch themselves are doing, when they are not watching television.

Sex

The Dutch preference for openness and clarity turns a bright light on to what is, for many other nations, the murky domain of sex. The English, in particular, are startled by the glare. But, as it is such a lights-on affair, sex is, for the Dutch, as much part of the clear world of reason as of the trickier realms of passion. A bordello in southern Holland advertises special days set aside for people with physical disabilities. A fully clothed television announcer can talk freely about the necessity for safe sex against the seething backdrop of a 'Safe Sex Orgy', filmed live. The shaven-headed leader of a sadomasochists' club is interviewed (in bed), not about what its members get up to, but about how the club is organized.

66 One national magazine runs a popular column in which couples pose naked and frankly discuss each other's physical attributes. 99

When it comes to personal relationships, the Dutch are just as open. One national magazine runs a popular column in which couples pose naked (heads and surnames blotted out) and frankly discuss each other's physical attributes. The most popular television programmes are those in which couples that have split up are reconciled (or not, as the case may be) in full view of the nation.

Sense of Humour

The Dutch sense of humour relishes mishap and mayhem, rather than verbal acrobatics. Someone falling through his chair on to the floor will get a bigger laugh than the bravest pun. Uncle Theo disappearing and coming back in Aunt Miep's frock goes down a great deal better than attempts at witty banter around the dinner table. Running through all this knockabout jollity is a tough, cruel streak. A good dollop of suffering and humiliation will have a Dutch audience on its knees with mirth. Despite their disdain for most things German, the Dutch revel in *Schadenfreude*.

A whiff of naughtiness and the violation of the odd taboo are also common ingredients for a good laugh. If they weren't so wary of being politically incorrect, the Dutch would adore Benny Hill. Many secretly do.

The more refined brands of Dutch humour are dry, and delight in absurdity and in turning social values topsy turvy. At times this becomes

> **A good dollop of suffering and humiliation will have a Dutch audience on its knees with mirth.**

a gentle national whimsy, of the sort that results in city councils having trams covered in cartoons and bright designs, but there are strains of this humour that can leave the foreigner nonplussed: "Good God!" cries a nouveau riche, eyeing his hostess's cocktail frock and bringing party conversation to a halt: "What a fine fabric. It would make a wonderful dress!"

Dutch people are too frank to dabble in irony. They will take what you say at face value and interpret your carefully honed ironies as error, insult or sarcasm. But they do share with the English an ability to laugh at themselves – "How was copper wire invented?" "By two Dutchmen fighting over a *stuiver* [a copper 5c piece]".

Eating & Drinking

What is sold where

Hypermarkets, megamarkets and maximarts beckon, but large-scale, impersonal shopping is not really the Dutch way. Small, specialized, neighbourhood stores are more *gezellig*, and the local street-market is probably cheaper. Most people buy supplies daily, rather than in plasti-wrapped bulk, and look forward to having a chat and maybe even a cup of coffee while they are about it.

> 66 When it's their turn to be served they expect to be allowed all the time in the world to pick and choose and pass the time of day. 99

The Dutch cheerily greet the shopkeeper as they come in, and leave with a friendly "*Tot ziens*" ('See you again'). When it's their turn to be served they expect to be allowed all the time in the world to pick and choose and pass the time of day. Tasting your cheese before you buy it, asking the cheeseshop assistant's advice, and deciding whether you want a wedge or a flat cut, is all part of the enjoyment. Outside the shops, brightly painted street organs pipe tunes that give a festive air to an ordinary activity.

Local trades unions have put a ceiling on weekly opening hours. Shops in the Netherlands stay open on Saturday afternoons, choose whether or not to open on Sunday, and close on Monday mornings, when few people could be much bothered to visit them anyway.

After hours, you will find anything from *chorizo* to champagne at the neighbourhood 'night shop', which opens just as other shops close. Fresh flowers – items essential to Dutch social intercourse – are on sale at all times of night and day from roadside kiosks, night shops and even petrol stations. Coffee, another staple, can be found in the most unexpected places, including the butcher's.

The feast

Erasmus, the great 16th-century Dutch humanist and man of letters, noted that his countrymen 'were not prone to any serious vices except, that is, a little given to pleasure, especially to feasting'. Four centuries later the national ability to tuck in and drink up is still impressive. Quantity is as important as quality in Dutch cooking. The

> **66** The national ability to tuck in and drink up is impressive. Quantity is as important as quality in Dutch cooking. **99**

national dish, *hutspot* ('hotchpotch'), is a well-boiled stew that was fed to starving citizens after the siege of the city of Leiden, and still requires a similar state of ravenousness before it can be truly appreciated.

The Dutch breakfast will consist of coffee (in abundance), bread, cheese, flaked chocolate (to scatter on the bread, and thence over the whole table), and just one more cup of coffee. Lunch comprises coffee and a *broodje* – a bread roll with cheese or ham, or served *gezond* ('healthy' – layered with cholesterol-rich cheese, the odd lettuce leaf and an egg thrown in for good measure). In addition to the coffee there will be a good, healthy glass of milk – or better still, thick buttermilk.

> **Curiously, in this land of milk and cheese the only cream that is ever available is thin and watery, or aerated into a tasteless froth.**

There are one or two coffee breaks in between. Midway through the afternoon you might meet up with a friend for a cup of coffee, in which case you may lash out on a little *gebakje* – usually a slice of apple tart with cream. Curiously, in this land of milk and cheese the only cream that is ever available is thin and watery, or aerated into a tasteless froth. Dinner is early, at around 6 or 7 o'clock, to give you time to pop down to your local café for a beer or a cup of coffee later on.

In between meals the Dutch devour large quantities of potato chips smothered in mayonnaise or, if they are really peckish, served *oorlog* (literally 'war'), i.e., spattered with ketchup, mayonnaise and one or two other sauces as well. Alternatively, they stop off at a roadside kiosk for a quick raw herring. These are eaten by holding it by the tail, tossing your head back and slipping a whole fillet down your throat. It's an experience that few foreigners voluntarily undergo.

Killing vegetables

The Belgians fry, the Germans pickle, the English boil, and the Dutch mash – cabbages and potatoes especially, but also endives and peas all end up pounded together in a stolid *stamppot*. Usually greyish-white in hue, with green flecks and the consistency of partially set concrete, *stamppot* is dished up with something meaty.

In traditional Dutch cuisine no meal is considered complete without meat. Even pea soup (which is expected to be so thick that you can stand your spoon upright in it) comes with floating sausages and bacon. Fish has honorary status as a vegetable: the 'vegetarian' section of a menu in a traditional Dutch restaurant will invariably involve cod. In a Dutch household the question "What's for dinner?" gets the answer "Broccoli", or "Spinach", or whatever else the main vegetable is that night. Meat is a given, not a variable.

> **In traditional Dutch cuisine no meal is considered complete without meat. Even pea soup comes with floating sausages and bacon.**

Not even salads escape the masher. A Dutch salad is 90% potato and mayonnaise, and 10% something else that gives it a name rather than a flavour. Consequently, most salads are creamy white and are only distinguishable from each other by the label. Innovations in the field have added virulent yellow (chicken curry salad) and a pale pink (prawn) to the spectrum.

Foreign flavours

'Fusion cuisine' was a standard in the Netherlands years before it became trendy elsewhere in Europe. Traditional Dutch cuisine, like Dutch culture, has recreated itself as a sort of mix-and-match of foreign influences. France was raided first, then the ex-colonies in Indonesia, followed by the Mediterranean and the Orient. British celebrity chefs have made an impact, too, via cabled BBC TV. A 'New Dutch Cuisine' has developed which offers such delights as apple cannelloni with smoked eel and a dab of foie gras.

66 Chefs of cuisines noted for the delicacy of their portions, such as the Japanese, have learned to serve larger helpings and add more beef to the menu. 99

Brave attempts by foreign cuisines to fight back have met with some success. Ethnic restaurants abound, but are suitably tempered to Dutch taste. Curries differ from stew in colour only, and chefs of cuisines noted for the delicacy of their portions, such as the Japanese, have learned to serve larger helpings and add more beef to the menu. Nouvelle cuisine was never a great success in the Netherlands. Besides offering mingy portions it gave bad value for money.

The most popular foreign meal by far is the Indonesian *rijsttafel*, a personal banquet of rice with a host of side dishes that appeals to the Dutch instinct for feasting. The *rijsttafel* originated in colonial times when Dutch settlers in Indonesia found local servings too meagre, and inventive cooks responded by placing the entire contents of the larder on the table.

Drinking

When they are not drinking coffee, the Dutch put away enormous quantities of beer, though they do so genteelly, sipping at fluted glasses that hold just a mouthful or two. Serious drinkers hurry things along with a gin chaser, calling the combination a *kopstoot* ('headbanger').

Jenever, the ancestor of British gin, was invented by a Dutch doctor as a diuretic and retains a medicinal tang. It comes in a small glass filled

> **Gin comes in a small glass filled to the brim, so that the first sip has to be taken by lowering your chin to the table.**

to the brim, so that the first sip has to be taken by lowering your chin to the table. Then you knock back the rest with a single gulp. If you are lucky, you might get the *Amsterdammertje*: if the last bit of *jenever* in the bottle doesn't quite fill the glass, then you down it for free and get a refill. *Jenever* comes *oud* (old and mellow) or *jong* (young and sharp), and sometimes in lemon or blackberry flavours.

Advocaat is a more idiosyncratic drink, and very much an acquired taste. A sort of alcoholic custard made from raw eggs and cognac, it comes in a glass, but is best tackled with a spoon and makes more sense as a sauce poured over ice-cream.

The favoured place for drinking is a 'brown café' (that is, one where the walls and ceiling have been stained by decades of tobacco smoke), though on freezing winter's days the Dutch will warm their blood with a quick visit to a *proeflokaal*. These were once free tasting houses attached to a *jenever* merchant's premises. These days you have to pay, but the procedure is much the same: walk in, drink up, walk out.

> **Endless cups of coffee, frequent nibbles on biscuits and slices of fatty cheese can take their toll on arteries and veins.**

Health & Hygiene

Endless cups of coffee, frequent nibbles on biscuits and slices of fatty cheese can take their toll on arteries and veins. Yet, although heart disease is the Netherlands' number one killer, the Dutch are a sturdy bunch who manage to live longer, on average, than any other Europeans. They put this down to a natural healthiness they inherited from their robust farmer ancestors, and continue to tuck in.

A Dutch doctor's invariable advice on a first visit is for the patient to wait and see how things turn out, to

"Let nature take its course" and allow the body to heal itself (seemingly incognisant of the fact that the general course of nature is towards death, and that a doctor's job is to intervene). Foreigners are scandalized, often with justification when ailments turn out to be something serious. They might take comfort in the thought that they could very possibly train up for the job themselves, for in this egalitarian country entry to study in medical school is based on a lottery system, rather than on ability.

> **66 Nearly half the nation's babies are born at home, and few Dutch mothers use any sort of anaesthetic or painkiller during the delivery. 99**

If their doctors believe in the inherently hardy constitutions of their patients, Dutch women take a similarly natural approach to childbirth. Nearly half the nation's babies are born at home, and few Dutch mothers use any sort of anaesthetic or painkiller during the delivery. Even mothers who have their babies in hospital are packed off home after a day or two, sometimes within hours. Nature and a recent international survey on childbirth approve – the Netherlands is one of the safest places on earth to have a baby.

Teeth, on the other hand, are a subject of great concern. Dentists drill and fill, but each practice also has a 'Mouth Hygienist', whose task it is to carry on the time-honoured Dutch activities of scrubbing,

61

scraping, buffing and polishing. Costs pile up, and the health insurance won't always foot the bill. All this trouble and expense does not leave the Dutch with straight, glistening, American-style grins. As in their battle against the ocean, all the hard work simply serves to keep things functional and intact.

Though they will spend hours cleaning their houses, the Dutch prefer to get their personal ablutions out of the way as speedily as possible. Showers win out over baths as they are quicker and cheaper to operate. Bathrooms are small. In many you could shower and use the lavatory simultaneously, thus saving even more time. Sometimes there isn't even room for a basin, forcing people to shave and clean their teeth over the kitchen sink. This is not a problem in a Dutch household, as there are never any dirty dishes lying around.

> **Bathrooms are small. In many you could shower and use the lavatory simultaneously.**

The cleaning of teeth is the only part of the process over which the Dutch may linger, but here time is seen as an investment against outrageous dentists' bills. An armoury of brushes, wooden spikes, mirrors on sticks and metal scrapers all help in the battle against plaque and the ravages of caffeine. These line up alongside the bottles of homeopathic medicines (paid for by health insurance) which help nudge nature along her course when she is proving reluctant. The odd potion or balm inherited (together with all those healthy genes) from rural ancestors also makes an appearance – *uierzalf*, a soothing balm made for cows' udders, is a particular favourite.

Custom & Tradition

The Dutch jump at any excuse to hang out the bunting. Important football matches and national holidays are the best reasons of all. Trams have fittings on the front to which the driver can attach flags for special occasions, and most houses are equipped with their own pole-holders. Even a celebratory picnic in the park involves stringing lines of brightly coloured pennants between the trees.

The jolliest national holiday is *Koninginnedag* – the Queen's official birthday, at the end of April.

> **" Trams have fittings on the front to which the driver can attach flags for special occasions, and most houses are equipped with their own pole-holders. "**

This the Dutch celebrate in good mercantile style by holding an enormous fleamarket. Anyone can sell anything anywhere. National flags, yards of orange cloth (for the House of Orange) and pretty pennants decorate the buildings. Cafés move their business outdoors, *gezelligheid* bursts all bounds and people party in the streets the whole day long. Although millions do this, everything sails smoothly along with impeccable Dutch control and an understanding of how to have a good time without upsetting the neighbours.

Not so New Year's Eve, when the point is to terrify as many people as you can with fireworks. Youths lurk in dark doorways to throw crackers at your feet, wags set off whole boxes at once and improvise with tins and bottles to make louder bangs (often maiming themselves in the process). By midnight a cloud of gunpowder smoke hangs over the country and the Netherlands flashes and explodes like a battleground.

> **66 By midnight a cloud of gunpowder smoke hangs over the country and the Netherlands flashes and explodes like a battleground. 99**

Christmas, on the other hand, is a low-key affair. Traditionally, it is *Sinterklaas*, St. Nicholas's day on 6th December, that attracts most festivity. For weeks beforehand, genial, white-haired St. Nicholases traipse through the Netherlands with a servant, Black Pete, in tow. Black Pete is usually a white person with layers of dark make-up, a fuzzy wig and big red lips. Children are told that he will come in the night and take them away if they are naughty. Curiously, the Dutch see nothing insulting or disturbing in this. The chat show guests who are assembled to discuss the racist implications usually bow to the claims of Tradition. Attempts to undermine the custom –

White Pete (a black person with chalky make-up), Green Pete (environmental lobby) and Pink Pete (gay) – usually fall flat. People will explain away Black Pete as a white child who has been delivering presents down the chimney.

Sinterklaas himself is the forerunner of Santa Claus. The re-importation of the tubby man in red on 25th December has lead to some confusion among Dutch children, who are told that he is Sinterklaas's brother. Even though he is a Catholic saint, Sinterklaas survived even the most fervently Protestant moments of the Netherlands' history. But perhaps that is because anyone bearing free gifts is a welcome guest in a Dutch home.

On the evening of 5th December, Dutch families gather to eat chewy gingerbread and other *Sinterklaas* fare and to swap presents.

> **66 The gifts are simple, inexpensive and usually make some point about the recipient's character or behaviour. 99**

The gifts are simple, inexpensive and usually make some point about the recipient's character or behaviour. They are accompanied by a poem, penned by the giver, that drives the point home. Less robust nations might think that giving someone a stick of deodorant, with a few neatly rhymed couplets about her bathing habits, is the sort of activity that is bound to end in tears, but to the forthright Dutch it is all a recipe for a jolly good time.

Rites of passage

Some 20% of Dutch adults live alone. In certain parts of the country around 50% of households are made up of single people, and only 12% of homes contain two-parent families. A good many others live together as couples with no social stigma at all, and people who co-habit for five years or more are afforded the same social and tax advantages as married couples. Though marriage is respectable, most Dutch parents would prefer their offspring to live together with someone for a few years than to marry young.

> **When people do decide to get married they often have two weddings – one in the town hall (to legalise the bond) and one in church (for show).**

When people do decide to get married they often have two weddings – one in the town hall (to legalise the bond) and one in church (for show). From the legal point of view, a wedding that takes place in church only does not count. There are also two receptions – a large formal dinner for all the guests, and a subsequent riotous bash for favoured friends. As with many things in Dutch life, propriety and wantonness go hand-in-hand.

Dutch forthrightness dictates that invitations should specify whether or not you are invited to the second party. This gives rise to the most anguished social decision that most Dutch people are ever called on to make. People who thought themselves close friends may be lost for life if they come down on the wrong side of the great divide.

The Dutch say that a wedding starts with glamour, and ends in underwear. This doesn't refer so much to the happy couple, as to the guests at the second party. As the alcohol begins to flow, the sing-along and silly dances begin and the feast becomes Bacchanalian. From time to time a couple of guests disappear for a few minutes and return in costume to act out an (apparently) hilarious sketch. The butt of all these dramatic offerings is the newly wedded couple – their bad habits, repellent quirks and previous amours.

Understandably, funerals are a little more sedate, though generally fairly secular in timbre. Family and friends head off to the *Uitvaartcentrum* ('departure centre'), where the loved one is dispatched to the sound of music (*My Way* and songs by Mieke Telkamp, the Dutch Vera Lynn, are perennial favourites). Afterwards everyone gathers in an ante-chamber for coffee and one slice of cake.

> **66** The only sin in the Dutch canon is to forget somebody's birthday. Every Dutch lavatory has a birthday calendar pinned to the back of the door. **99**

The only utterly unforgivable sin in the Dutch canon is to forget somebody's birthday. Every Dutch lavatory has a birthday calendar pinned to the back of the door, so that inhabitants of the house can be sure that they will get a daily reminder of their friends' and relations' big day. Birthdays are the pivot of a Dutch person's internal calendar, and the ritual of their celebration is always the same. Close friends and family come for coffee. They will bring flowers, and sometimes a small gift. They will expect to sit in a circle, make polite conversation, sip their coffee and eat their slice of cake. In this they will not be disappointed, though in honour of the occasion a second slice of cake may be offered. There will be colourful paper chains overhead, and flags. A glass of port or sherry will be served to signal the end of the proceedings.

❝ Dutch life runs with a quiet efficiency. They are not ostentatious about achieving this order. ❞

Systems

Dutch life runs with a quiet efficiency. Streets are cleaned and letters are delivered the day after they are posted, without any fuss, simply as a matter of course. Unlike the Germans, the Dutch are not osten-tatious about achieving this order, nor are their sys-tems fettered by tradition, like those of the English.

A good example is the system employed when the Rolling Stones announced an impromptu concert in Amsterdam in a hall which could accommodate just 1,200 eager fans. The organisers let it be known that there were three possible ticket outlets, but that only one of them at the given hour would actually have tickets on sale. As the points chosen were sufficiently far apart, this not only prevented a large queue forming at one place, but instantly reduced the numbers by two-thirds. Then, the box office which was doing business with the lucky ones, instead of issuing tickets, gave out plastic bracelets, which would break if removed. In this way only those who had gone to the trouble of queuing could get into the concert, and there was no temptation (indeed, no possibility) of reselling tickets at a substantial profit.

Good organization helps make life *gezellig*, and is worth whatever it costs (though it doesn't do to flaunt your success at it), and changes that improve old ways are readily accepted.

Respectable citizens participate in life's systems – public and private – with honesty. They run up tabs at the bar, and don't disappear without paying; they

> **66 Good organization is worth whatever it costs, and changes that improve old ways are readily accepted. 99**

pay their taxes without too much fuss, and frank their own tickets on public transport. People who break this trust can expect to feel the full thrust of social and legal disapprobation. 'Black riders' (or 'grey riders' to the politically correct) who are caught without a valid ticket have to pay an on-the-spot fine that amounts to twenty times the normal fare. If they don't have the money – or some form of identification – on them, doors are sealed and everything comes to a halt while the police are called. Respectable citizens then disapprove even more strongly because they have been made late, and punctuality is fundamental to the smooth running of things.

The not so open road

As the Netherlands is so small and overcrowded, roads have to be squeezed in as best they can. Traffic signs occur every few yards, turning trips across cities into a staccato of stops and starts, and suggesting all sorts of contradictory directions for longer journeys.

66 As the Netherlands is so small and overcrowded, roads have to be squeezed in as best they can. 99

The Dutch are not confused by this: once meshed into the knot of motorways they know that they are bound to turn up at their destination sooner or later. If they miss a turning there is sure to be another one further on and, besides, it takes about as much time to cross the entire country as it takes people in London or Berlin to get to work. Yet there are signs that the pace of modern life is taking its toll. Road rage in the Netherlands has increased alarmingly in recent years, as more and more people join the squeeze.

Education

Less than a third of Dutch schoolchildren attend conventional state schools. Perhaps that is why a survey carried out by the World Health Organization found Dutch schoolchildren to be the happiest out of all those in Europe and northern America. Most of them go to schools specific to one of the three *zuilen* – Protestant, Roman Catholic or Montessori/Alternative (or, increasingly, so-called 'Black' schools comprising mainly children of immigrants). Though privately run, these establishments get state subsidies, and all children sit the same state exams. The idea of an elite crust of private schools is anathema to the egalitarian Dutch, and if you gather together a sufficient number of children in the name of education, the Dutch government will allow you (subject to the usual rules and regulations and ties of bureaucracy) to start up a school of your own.

> **❝ The Dutch respect a good education and see it as the first step in the process of taking your place in society. ❞**

Specialization starts early. When they enter secondary school, at around the age of 12, children are channelled into a course which leads to university, or in the direction of a career qualification.

The Dutch respect a good education and see it as the first step in the process of taking your place in society, shouldering your part of the burden of hard work and earning your just reward. Those that have a university degree do not flaunt it, but feel quite happy at adding the letters to their name on business cards, or being addressed on envelopes as Drs (short for *Doctorandus*, and not to be confused with the 'Dr' earned by those who have a doctorate). People with law degrees style themselves *Meester* (shortened to 'Mr'), in addition to any other title they have. This goes for women too – 'Mrs Mr Smit'.

The Dutch have reason to consider themselves well-educated: over 20% have been to university or college (compared with 15% of the French population and 4% in Portugal). Get into a conversation about T.S. Eliot, Nietzsche or Proust, and the chances are that a Dutch person

> **❝ Get into a conversation about T.S. Eliot, Nietzsche or Proust, and the chances are that a Dutch person will have read the lot in the original language. ❞**

will have read the lot in the original language – or will at least be convinced that he or she has an innate ability to express an opinion on them.

For many years tertiary education provided a convenient stop gap for schoolboys unwilling to step off the playground straight on to the parade ground. But in 1996 national military service was abolished in the Netherlands. Lawyers who had specialized in getting young men off the hook lost a steady source of income. Regular army officers, on the other hand, gleefully took the opportunity to repeal all the namby-pamby regulations which had allowed soldiers to have long hair and wear earrings. Yet even here the Dutch refusal to take officialdom too seriously gave the event a wry edge. As a memento, the last intake of servicemen were each given a Walkman with a cassette of a sergeant-major barking drill orders.

Crime & Punishment

The Dutch combine two qualities which most other nations find mutually exclusive – regulated efficiency and laissez-faire. The Italians blatantly break rules, the Germans apply them obsessively in the quest for *Ordnung*. The English bicker for ages over the niceties of regulations, then heed them to the letter. The Dutch will enforce a law when it seems sensible to do so, and ignore it when it does not. All officials have one blind eye and a permanent crick in the neck.

> **The Dutch will enforce a law when it seems sensible to do so, and ignore it when it does not. All officials have one blind eye and a permanent crick in the neck.**

Contrary to popular belief, selling marijuana is not legal in the Netherlands. This, and many such activities, are *gedoogd* – not legal but nevertheless 'allowed' in certain controlled areas, to reduce the crime and nastiness that often surround them – another example of the Dutch letting in a little evil to keep out the bigger one.

This official blind eye was required to close even further when a smoking ban was introduced in restaurants and cafés across the country. Not being able to smoke rather defeats the purpose of marijuana 'coffeeshops', so again an exception was made: smoking is *gedoogd* in coffeeshops, providing it does not involve tobacco.

In like manner, most Dutch people will agree that it is simply common sense to allow prostitutes to work openly, protected from pimps and with access to free medical check-ups. In the Netherlands, prostitutes find themselves at loggerheads not with the moralists or the Law, but with feminists, who feel that they are letting the side down.

> **66 Dutch police publish details in the local press of when and where they'll be setting up speed traps so that casual offenders can take care not to get caught. 99**

When the Dutch tax office decided it was time to crack down on illegal workers in bars and cafés, the inspectors, in the spirit of fair play, published the dates of their 'raids' well in advance. This allowed small-time moonlighters to lie low, and meant that only establishments that had been cooking the books in a big way, and who couldn't possibly disguise the fact, got caught. Similarly, Dutch police publish details in the local press of when and where they'll be setting up speed traps so that casual kilometre-or-two-over the-limit offenders can take care not to get caught.

Prisons

Convicts languishing in Greek gaols, or stuffed into cells in Britain, dream of Dutch prisons. Yet, not satisfied with cable television, conjugal visiting rights and other comforts, Dutch prisoners have been known to complain about the unfriendliness of the guards, or that the food is fattening.

Dutch prisons are so popular that they have waiting lists of applicants for cells. Unless someone has committed a particularly heinous crime, they will be sentenced to community service, or be issued with a slip of paper which, rather like the tickets in the post-office queue, puts them in line for the next cell available.

> **❝ Not satisfied with cable television, conjugal visiting rights and other comforts, Dutch prisoners have been known to complain that the food is fattening. ❞**

The police

The Dutch police come in all colours and genders, and can be found in pairs, clad in trendy bomber jackets and well-cut trousers, often on mountain bikes, sometimes on horses, but generally as a background presence. Everybody is so busy being neighbourly, tolerant, *gezellig* and generally well-behaved that the police are pretty much left free to pursue hard-drugs dealers and other vicious criminals.

The liberal Dutch attitude towards cannabis does not extend to hard drugs, but it does attract 'drug tourists' to the Netherlands. Although the Dutch have the lowest number of hard-drug addicts per capita in Europe, large cities are nevertheless left with a drugs problem, which manifests itself mainly in petty theft. True to the Dutch spirit of seeing both sides of a problem, the police initiated

> 66 Bicycle theft is a national pastime. The Dutch spend more on hefty, supposedly foolproof locks than they do on the cycle itself. 99

legislation making it illegal to leave your car unlocked, or unattended with the keys in the ignition.

Bicycle theft is a national pastime. The Dutch spend more on hefty, supposedly foolproof locks than they do on the cycle itself. When a bicycle is stolen it is the loss of the lock that is most lamented. A replacement bicycle is easily come by – simply walk up to a group of cyclists and say loudly and authoritatively "That's *my* bike!". Someone is sure to get off and run away.

Business

The Dutch invented the multi-national. The V.O.C. (Dutch East India Company) was, for two centuries, the largest and most powerful trade organization in the world. Today Philips, Unilever and Royal Dutch Shell (together with two other companies that are not household names) employ a quarter of the Netherlands' workforce. The Dutch don't stop here, but export managers to take control of foreign multi-nationals. Their linguistic and negotiating prowess, as well as an ability to keep a tight control on the purse strings, quickly propel them to the top of the board.

> **True to the spirit of their trading forefathers, the Dutch remain adept middlemen, deftly turning around other people's products to make a profit.**

Dutch merchant ships have given way to pantechnicons – 40% of all international trucking in Europe is Dutch operated. True to the spirit of their trading forefathers, the Dutch remain adept middlemen, deftly turning around other people's products to make a profit. They import chemicals to make fertilizer, then use gas (their sole natural resource) to heat vast greenhouses that supply the markets of Europe with tomatoes, cucumbers, tulips, carnations, freesias and much more. Over 60% of the world's cut flowers and 50% of its pot plants pass through the Netherlands' gigantic auction houses, though not all of them are homegrown. The Dutch have such a hold on the market that, in order to realise the best prices, farmers in other countries send their blooms to the Netherlands to be sold – for the florist up the road to re-import them.

> **❝A visiting businessperson who is used to expense account lunches, will be sorely disappointed in the Netherlands.❞**

Dutch openness extends to the Dutch economy. Making too much fuss about regulations and restrictions is bad for trade, and the financial market is no exception to the rule. Centuries ago, the Amsterdam Bank of Exchange was the biggest commercial bank in the world. Foreign monarchs used it for loans to finance their military campaigns, and to stash away nest eggs in case they were toppled from power. Today, efficient transport links and the locals' facility with languages still attract foreign investors, though the tax incentives are no longer quite so generous and can change without warning.

Dutch frugality appears in business as well as in private life. A visiting businessperson who is used to expense account lunches, will be sorely disappointed in the Netherlands. Anything more than coffee and a cheese *broodje* is viewed as needlessly extravagant and a waste of time. Business hours are for business. Similarly, offices are modest to the point of austerity, and even letterheads and logos are suitably subdued.

Bosses and workers

The key word in a Dutch company is teamwork. Dutch business, like Dutch countryside, is organized horizontally rather than vertically. Co-operation, negotiation and consensus opinion are the mainspring of Dutch business. Endless meetings are their result. Like cafés, meetings provide ample ground for the exercising of opinions. The difference is that in a meeting the speakers must back their opinions with careful and comprehensive research. This gives them the confidence to express their opinions with an energy and resolution that other nations might find intimidating. But, in the end, there is a lot of give and take. The aim of a meeting is not to outvote a minority, but to reach a joint decision that the team can happily implement. Foreigners less used to such forthright cut and thrust, however, may be left bleeding by the wayside.

> **66 Co-operation, negotiation and consensus opinion are the mainspring of Dutch business. Endless meetings are their result. 99**

Rigid hierarchies are contrary to team spirit, and don't fit in with the Dutch view of an egalitarian society. Everyone from the office cleaner to the managing director is a company *medewerker* – a 'co-worker'. In a Dutch company, supervisors are 'co-ordinators' and, though the boss might be addressed as *U*, he – or she – knows better than even to think of issuing anything that might be taken to resemble an order. When industrial action does occur, it is often carried out in as *gezellig* a manner possible. During a train strike, workers decided that only the ticket inspectors (and not the drivers as well) would down tools. This was widely publicized, and meant that trains continued to run, and passengers knew they could ride for free. So the strikers made their point without disrupting the public, while hitting their bosses where it hurt – in the pocket.

> **❝ Dutch people cite 'ambition' as the second most important criterion (after hard work and ahead of education) for getting on in life. ❞**

One-upmanship and flaunting your individual abilities will alienate members of the team, and are not the way to go about getting promotion. That comes through hard work, a good co-operative spirit and the right education. Decisions made at the beginning of secondary school about which educational channel to follow, set Dutch workers on a course for life. Few people make it from the factory floor to the accounts department, let alone the boardroom.

On the other hand, Dutch people cite 'ambition' as the second most important criterion (after hard work and ahead of education) for getting on in life. Overt parading of your superiority might be unacceptable, but behind-the-scenes schemes and stratagems are just as complex and as effective in Dutch companies as in any others. Subtle signs stake out one's progress: the Dutch dress informally at work. Jeans and open-necked shirts are quite acceptable male attire. Dark suits are the preserve of very top management. Jeans combined with a jacket and tie mark the first step towards higher things. Next, jeans are dropped in favour of proper trousers. This sartorial signalling is subtly controlled. Dressing above one's station is contrary to good team spirit.

Even though the separation of workers and management is the closest that Dutch society comes to a class system, industrial relations are good. Negotiations between trades unions and management are non-confrontational. The law (and not only the ethos of teamwork) dictates that companies employing more than 35 people should set up an *ondernemingsraad* – a workers' council that has to be consulted on all major policy changes and on any matter relating to personnel. Even in smaller organizations, the workers are entitled to hold meetings twice a year in order to question the board about the running of the company. Outside office hours these divisions dissolve, and *medewerkers* are quite happy to wander down to the café and become *mede-*drinkers.

> **Sartorial signalling is subtly controlled. Dressing above one's station is contrary to good team spirit.**

Government & Bureaucracy

Unlike most other nations whose governments form a distant and detested caste, the Dutch tend to respect their politicians, and to trust them. Cabinet ministers and city burgomasters wield tremendous executive power, but the Dutch see them as 'one of us', important cogs in an egalitarian machine.

This does lead to a very managerial society, where authorities may instruct people how to live (for example, whether or not they may buy a house in a certain city, or rent one of a certain size) and the people mildly obey. Politicians change important rules, such as those relating to health care, housing or taxation, with an arbitariness and lack of consultation that other democratic nations simply would not tolerate, and everyone settles down quietly to obey the new law, as if some Great Mother had instructed *"Doe maar gewoon"* (Just behave). On the rare occasions that the populace rebels – such as in the Dutch rejection by referendum of a pan-European constitution – they shock not only their leaders but themselves as well, like children who know they have been very naughty and are rather in awe of their new-found power.

> **On the rare occasions that the populace rebels, they shock not only their leaders but themselves as well, like children who have been very naughty.**

Surprisingly in the Netherlands, where democracy and egalitarianism are so important, the Queen has a hands-on role in government. The sovereign is not just a figurehead to be dressed up and wheeled out to snip at ribbons and break champagne bottles over the bows of ships; she turns up for work daily and enjoys widespread respect.

Cabinet ministers are appointed by the Queen and have the right to speak, but not vote, in the Dutch Parliament (which is called the States-General and consists of an elected Lower and Upper House). Legislation starts

> **❝ Surprisingly in the Netherlands, where democracy and egalitarianism are so important, the Queen has a hands-on role in government. ❞**

at the top with the relevant Cabinet minister and passes downwards for approval by Parliament more often than the other way around. In cities, power is also centralised, with mayors (who are appointed rather than elected) holding extraordinary sway.

There is a saying that if you put two Dutch people in a room they will start a debate; add a third and they will found a church or a political party. Dutch tolerance and the belief in giving everybody a hearing gives the Netherlands an abundance of political parties. Proportional representation at elections means that many of them win seats in parliament. Yet the States-General is not a bicker box. Members of Parliament spend their time not at each other's throats, but in the time-honoured occupations of negotiation, compromise and working out coalition governments.

These days the sense of happy participation extends as far as a website that enables everyone in the country to vote on issues currently being debated in parliament – though of course the votes have no official status, and the well-behaved populace, once they have had their say, do what their leaders tell them.

Bureaucracy

For the person-in-the-street, tolerance and negotiation come to a juddering halt against a single phrase: *"Dat kan niet"* ('That is not possible'). Dutch people know that when they hear these words, it is time to give up and go home. *Dat kan niet* is the ultimate weapon of minor officials and dedicated bureaucrats.

> **66** Tolerance and negotiation come to a juddering halt against a single phrase: *"Dat kan niet"* ('That is not possible'). **99**

Like armies, bureaucracies the world over attract similar personalities. Dutch people who feel ill at ease with the national inclination towards flexibility dream of a job in the corridors of petty power. And once they have set their heart on something, they do it well. They learn *Catch 22* off pat, take out the red tape and prepare to tie you in knots. If you catch them off guard, spot a loophole, or try to introduce an element of rationality into your relationship, they counter with *Dat kan niet* – and that's final.

Language

Adept traders though they be, the Dutch have found it hard to export their language. Its guttural 'g' has potential clients muttering about diseases of the throat, and foreign lips and tongues give out entirely when trying to wrap themselves around 'ui'. The English dismiss anything they find too baffling as 'Double Dutch'. Van Gogh knew all too well the problems that his mother tongue gave others, so he signed his paintings 'Vincent' in the hope that gallerists would find that easier to pronounce than his surname.

On the other hand, the Dutch have never been shy about importing words from other languages. In the Netherlands everyone stops work for the 'weekend', says 'sorry' if they bump into you and enjoys freshly squeezed *jus d'orange*. They are famously proficient at speaking languages other than their own, and even manage to make some improvements with their errors, such as when they talk of a 'crowdy' room, or

> 66 The Dutch are famously proficient at speaking languages other than their own. 99

the laborious task of 'ironating' clothes. Yet there has been a reaction to the feeling that English is swamping Dutch in the academic world and in commerce. As the nation works out a stricter definition of what it means to be Dutch, people are taking a defensive pride in their language – one minister going so far as to suggest legislation against residents of the Netherlands speaking foreign languages in public, so a Moroccan supermarket assistant could be forbidden to address a compatriot in Berber or French.

> **66 Assuming it would be a temporary measure, people thought up all sorts of odd surnames, such as *Hoogen-boezem* ('high-bosomed'). 99**

Occasionally the Dutch have found the inaccessibility of their language a convenient screen. When Napoleon invaded the Netherlands he forced the Dutch to adopt surnames – something not all of them had thought of doing. Those without had to adopt that extra name quick-smart and, assuming it would be a temporary measure and that once the invader had been sent packing they could resort to their old way of life, people thought up all sorts of odd names so that they could have a good laugh at the unwitting French officials' expense. But the joke backfired. Today there are families burdened with such names as *Naaktgeboren* ('born naked'), *Hoogen-boezem* ('high bosomed'), or *Poepjens* ('pooh-pooh').

You can hear variations of Dutch spoken in Belgium (Flemish, or *Vlaams*) and among the descendants of the Boers in South Africa (*Afrikaans*). Though they will tell you derisory jokes about the Belgians, the Dutch rather envy the soft, melodic tones of *Vlaams*. *Afrikaans*, on the other hand, sounds to their ears like archaic baby talk and will send the average Dutch person into fits of giggles.

> **❝ Dutch seems to have grown up out of the bogs and polders. ❞**

Historically, Dutch is related to German, though it lacks the Teutonic gloss and edge. It is a softer, comfier, muddier tongue that seems to have grown up out of the bogs and polders – a *gezellige* language. The Dutch take the hard edge off any number of words by adding the diminutive *tje* or *je*. Thus, in their cosy neighbourhood café they will order a *pilsje* in preference to a pils, and cash-dispensing machines will invite you to insert your *pasje*. Friends and family get the same treatment. There can be nothing more *gezellig* than sitting down to a *kopje koffie* with Aunty Truusje.

The Author

Rodney Bolt was born in Africa, and for many years had an Irish passport, a British driving licence and a Dutch residence permit. After living and working in Greece, England and Germany, he came to roost in Amsterdam, where such hybrid creatures still pass unnoticed, and even feel themselves at home. In his case, so much at home that in 2008 he became a naturalized Dutch citizen.

During the 1980s he ran a pub theatre in London, and has worked as a theatre director, English teacher, private tutor, letter-sorter and journalist. Now he makes his living from writing and travel-writing, having finally given up attempts to fend off the Dutch desire to produce novels. *History Play*, his first work of fiction, was published in 2004, and was followed two years later by a biography of Mozart's madcap librettist (*Lorenzo Da Ponte: The Adventures of Mozart's Librettist in the Old and New Worlds*).

He lives in an apartment where the curtains are never drawn, and where he has happily succumbed to many other Dutch cravings and habits (including a milk scraper), but he will never, ever get used to having a loo with a shelf in the bowl.

Xenophobe's® lingo learners

"Speak the lingo by speaking English."

The French

French politicians look smart because power itself is chic, attractive, seductive, and one should dress to look the part. The French electorate would never allow any government to intervene in their lives if it were shabbily dressed.

The Italians

Generally speaking, the Italians tend to look on the bright side of life – a positive outlook aptly illustrated by their touching salutation: 'May the saddest days of your future be the happiest days of your past.'

The Japanese

The Japanese are trained throughout their lives to read each others' minds. This means it is not necessary to have or to express an opinion. In fact for a Japanese woman to be called opinionated is worse than being called ugly. To call a man 'decisive' is just as bad.

The Irish

Apart from the sheer volume of words they produce, the Irish are also noted for the eloquence of their speech. The colourful phrase just comes to them naturally, like whiskers to a goat.

The Spanish

Anyone attempting to understand the Spanish must first of all recognise the fact that they do not consider anything important except total enjoyment. If it is not enjoyable it will be ignored.

The Greeks

The ancient sages carved 'Nothing in excess' and 'Know thyself' on the portals of the Delphic Oracle, in an attempt to persuade their fellow Greeks to curb their emotions. They were not heeded then any more than they are now.

Xenophobe's® Guides are available
as e-books from Amazon, iBookstore, and
other online sources, and via:

www.xenophobes.com

Xenophobe's® Guides print versions
can be purchased through online retailers
(Amazon, etc.) or via our web site:

www.xenophobes.com

In the US contact:
IPG Trafalgar Square, Chicago

toll free no: 1-800-888-4741
e-mail: orders@ipgbook.com

In the UK, contact Oval Books, London

telephone: +44 (0)20 7733 8585
e-mail: info@ovalbooks.com

Oval Books
5 St John's Buildings
Canterbury Crescent
London SW9 7QH

Oval Books accepts Visa and Mastercard and offers
FREE packing and postage on orders of more than
one book (to one address).

Xenophobe's®
Guides